Ain't Leavin' This House Rough Dried

Poems by Michael Poage

Kansas City   Spartan Press   Missouri

Spartan Press
Kansas City, Missouri
spartanpresskc.com

Copyright © Michael Poage, 2019
First Edition1 3 5 7 9 10 8 6 4 2
ISBN: 978-1-950380-61-9
LCCN: 2019949455

Design, edits and layout: Jason Ryberg
Cover and title page images: Jamie Rhodes
Author photo: Gretchen Eick
All rights reserved. No part of this publication may be reproduced or transmitted in any form or by any means, electronic or mechanical, including photocopying, recording or by info retrieval system, without prior written permission from the author.

ACKNOWLEDGMENTS

Grateful acknowledgment is made to the editors of the
following journals and anthologies, in which some of
these poems first appeared or were accepted for publication:

*The Café Review, Poetry East, Poetry Harbor, I-70 Review,
Ibbetson St. Press.*

"Back There" first appeared in the anthology: *The Wakarusa
Wetlands in Word and Image.*

"Night Jasmine" first appeared in the anthology: *Joyful Noise:
An Anthology of American Spiritual Poetry.*

TABLE OF CONTENTS

Lesson #1 / 1
A Night On Broadway / 2
Somewhere / 3
Future Home Of Glad Tidings Church / 4
Some Savior / 5
Blood Test / 6
Stealing "The Scream" / 7
Dear Edward / 8
No Child Left Behind / 9
O What Love / 10
Woman Regrets Killing Husband / 11
Stari Most / 12
Preacher / 13
Bethlehem / 14
Holding On / 15
The Smile / 16
But Who Can Endure…? / 17
The Prophet / 18
A Rose For Elleke / 19
The Deepest Water I Know / 20
Mass Grave / 21
How To / 22
The Divorce / 23
First Step / 24
Oboe Solo / 25
The Workout / 26
Constellation / 27

Postcard From Mexico / 28

Her Madness / 29

Sljivovica / 30

Concertina Wire / 31

There's More To Kansas / 32

Memorial Day / 33

Finally / 34

The Tijuana City Dump / 35

Being Zeus / 36

Roses / 37

"Crescendo In Blue" / 38

Near Miss / 40

Watching The News / 41

Woman Wins Gas For Life / 42

Ms. Taylor / 43

Night Jasmine / 44

Lesson #9 / 45

Lesson #10 / 46

Back There / 47

First Storm / 48

Whispering / 49

The Woman From Tyre / 50

Fiddling / 51

Bosnian Folk Song / 52

Dimming / 53

Glass / 54

Secrets / 55

Revenge / 56

A Cold Spring / 58

Last Therapy Before Bosnia / 59

I Dream Of Whining / 60

Late Winter / 61

The War Game / 62

Vigil / 63

Something About My Life / 64

January 25 / 65

End Rhyme / 67

My Surroundings (Part 1) / 68

The Noise Of Plants / 70

Hope / 71

The Dance / 72

Sarajevo Symphony / 73

Strange Fruit / 74

School In Sudan / 75

Not A Fairy Tale / 76

The House / 77

Weathered / 78

The Years / 79

Sunday's Comin' / 80

With respect, love and hope, I dedicate this book to my students at Dzemal Bijedic University, Mostar, Bosnia and Herzegovina.

She sang a slow song in a deep voice. They felt her misery rise, up the stairs, up through the wood and ceiling, clear up, they hoped, to sky's heaven.

—Linda Hogan, MEAN SPIRIT

LESSON #1

I trust no one
with my name
in their mouth.

A NIGHT ON BROADWAY

Ain't leavin' this house rough dried.
You put on the ironed skirt I fixed

for you last night and the good blouse
your Grandma gave you for church.

You ain't goin' outside with your hair
lookin' like steel wool from the hardware

store, you brush it down and out and do
your teeth while you're at it. And your face

ain't too good either with those
marks and cuts, you fix up those scars

or no man will want you. Then those
earrings need to go, put on the long

bright ones I got you in Vegas
cheap but they attract the money men

like dirt flies. Those lips need softenin'
so use this gloss from Walgreen's

just for your color and shape. Now
stand up straight. With those eyes

and hips and long fourteen year old
legs you bring me back some real gold.

SOMEWHERE

a left wrist bone is on the ground
next to a leg from a woman
waiting for bread just moments ago. A baby
blown from her mother's arms
is found crushed under a jeep
half a block down the street.
There are toes and ankles for the stray
dogs to steal. My job
is to get the other poor
bastard to die
for his country. We
are all doing well.

FUTURE HOME OF GLAD TIDINGS CHURCH

Bending your knees to the floor
you pray. After that you walk to a book store
for coffee and then wander into the
children's section. All the Easter
specials are on display but you find the classics that you
remember hearing and reading a lifetime ago. God played
with you then and made you laugh
and taught you games, words, how to sing,
both of you being just children.

SOME SAVIOR

This alley leads to a wall
with the message: To be saved,
you must shoot six times
into a small brown house,
the one on the corner of 16th
and Erie. Of course, only the select few
can read the ancient script. At 12:14 a.m.
it is Easter morning, the cross
has been carried, dropped,
carried again. The nails remain.
The women mourn and the men have disappeared
hours ago. It is time to go for a drive
looking for some savior's shadow
flickering like a candle
behind the curtained window
about to be shattered.

BLOOD TEST

The doctor called this morning
with the news – perfect blood,
vampire heaven, get out the cross
and the dagger. Tonight will be
wild on the town, we'll have to watch
everyone. Times Square is full of the stranger
and lovely, black-coated lovelies, with scarves
swirling like war-time snow. With perfect blood
you can be entertained, photographed, walk
the red carpet into posh blinding lights.

STEALING "THE SCREAM"
-- BOSNIA, 2004

I watch the men play chess
in Sarajevo. The pieces are large,
the size of the legless man
begging at the wall of the mosque.
He plays the accordion to attract
extra donations. It may be music
to the ears of thousands buried
in local football fields. It may not be music
at all to those who hate
the musician. And to those
involved in stealing "The Scream,"
that painting my granddaughter
copied in chalk for my refrigerator door,
the painting meant to haunt
the lives so many of us missed
by such remembrances. So
surrender now to the authorities
or we will take all
of your women and children,
put them in some sacred place,
tie their wrists behind
their backs and let
the building burn. On second thought
keep the painting and the music
will split your heart
like an ax to dry wood.

DEAR EDWARD

Thank you for the message
about your mother and
your life at the Boston
hospital. Some of it
sounds so familiar. The green
bile in the pan, the strength
in her dying smile, instructions
to give her the most
comfort possible. Today
I talked with a ten year old
girl from the next block whose
auntie was shot and killed
a few days ago. Brianna gave me
a hug and a smile, I responded
with same. I now pass Brianna's smile
and hug on to you. She would
approve. We all know something
about the green –
and there will be
other colors. The winter solstice
is coming, Hanukkah
began Saturday. Both
announce a change
in the light.

NO CHILD LEFT BEHIND

He has a shark smile as if he would lend
you anything. Put it all out on the table
so he can see it like a wound to tend

from crossing the seller at Piatt and 14th Street.
His name was never given, it was forced on him
by someone in the dark you would not want to meet.

Flesh to flesh, all those men gathered in their stoned way
with her young children all in one small room waiting
their turn at the television. But the men all stay

and use those children for the toys that crack
as they are opened. It is a quiet evening, a quiet
house, no one would know you took that pretty snack.

O WHAT LOVE

O what love does to an old heart.
From my study window

looking down on Hillside St.
I see the homecoming Escort vans,

the blue light specials flashing
their way through late morning traffic

leading a funeral procession. My first thought,
of course, should I have been officiating,

but only a few people I know have died in
the past few days, o what love. It is

the middle of Lent. What will Good Friday
bring you and me? Or later that weekend

we could hope for some ordinary
resurrection. You have a blood clot

in your leg that splits in two. Both pieces
go to the heart but because of the

brokenness you live.
The heart cannot take large

constrictions but perhaps small ones.
The broken blood has saved you.

WOMAN REGRETS KILLING HUSBAND

I was drunk and you know
what happens when
you get drunk. Tequila.
It was stupid. I did
a stupid thing. I loved
Roger. He was my future.
He has a good family.
Now I've lost everything. No
money. No family. I deserve
the most severe penalty
and the key thrown away.
We were just at home one evening
on the west side. He was tired,
drinking beer. I just walked
across the room to the closet,
brought out the shotgun
and pulled the trigger.
You know what happens.
Tequila by the grace of God.

STARI MOST

Mostar, Bosnia-Hercegovina

Beauty
is built from mistakes.
So from
the Neretva
all progress begins with
photographs, memory,
arguments
of residents,
on to the gathering
of tools and
stone. Any beautiful
bridge is
a human body
and now you
are lifting your broken
bones – leg, skull –
out of the water,
standing on your own,
solid finally from centuries
of longing to move
from one side
to the other.
It is a long walk
and we could lose
our balance.
This mistake, we fear,
may not last forever.

PREACHER

Drifting from here to there,
from the hotel to the street
preaching
corner to corner.
Women like that. They might give you
a meal
but not a room
for the night. Religion
is one thing, preaching
something else
again. So many of us
spend lives
with an eye
over our shoulder but you
decided: *God watches my back.*
My eyes are dead in front.

BETHLEHEM

I am doing my job.
Is it true
that advent is about God
not forgetting?
For nineteen years
people have been
coming to me with lives
dying as much as
could be expected.
But now
everyone has left
the building.
I will go soon,
get a glass of wine,
disappear into
my own quiet love,
a couch the color
of wheat, almost human,
manger-like,
without the star.

HOLDING ON

I like the idea of what
the rest of you deny
out of hatred and do
something good with it.
I'd like to live in the garden
although you may not. I'm afraid
I need directions
otherwise I may be lost —

otherwise — good title for
a book of poems

otherwise
I'm afraid.

THE SMILE

My grandson says
Hobby Lobby is evil. I agree.
You know it just by walking through
the doors, not hell exactly, but
a frightening place filled with beads,
plants that were never alive, paint by number,
green ware, racks of frames with photos
of smiling young girls whose fate
no one knows. The store clerks
remind me of characters in the old
zombie movies – pale, lifeless, eyes never
blinking. What is their life story? What debts
do they have? Will someone greet them
at home and say, "I love you?" Or is that
just a hobby we all practice from time
to time to make it to the next
person who smiles, seeming to like you,
and asks: *May I help?*

But who can endure…?
— Malachi 3:2

This is your face
at Christmas. The house
is so sensitive
and, in the photograph,
even looks like you.

Under the tinseled
tree you find your first
rifle. But you are not
sure if it is real
or another toy.

Soon you are
amazed by what
has been let
loose inside.

THE PROPHET

Jeremiah
reminds me
of my husband. He keeps
talking to me
after my eyes
are shut.

*My day went
like this…, and then
this happened…*

Then the damn angel
proclaimed:
Do not fear.
I say:
What kind
of advice
is that?

A ROSE FOR ELLEKE

Granddaughter, b. 9-22-03

This rose
bred for
red
has fragrance,
many,
for grace, gift
or gripe
as life begins
at seven pounds,
seven ounces
breaking the quiet
like diving
out of water.

THE DEEPEST WATER I KNOW

I am 58 years old
and eating tuna out of a can
for supper. I have
a real job
with health,
other benefits
and respect
at least from some.
So now
the wine.

MASS GRAVE

You have a special touch
with the dying. It's the living
that give you trouble. Maybe it is knowing
that death will take them
out of your danger zone into
a file folder with vital information
hand-written – year by year.
The living take a toll that keeps you
reaching into your pockets for change
and your heart pays forever. It was cold
from the north today like winter which it is
to the soul, to the bone. The body is an image
just below the earth like a photo
shuttered from the sky.

HOW TO

Being a parent, yes,
is hard. Being
a child,
nearly
impossible.

THE DIVORCE

I'm afraid of stuff.
Of sleeping and not.
The radio news and music in the dark and silence.
Being left behind when the adults are gone.
Your tears that make mine stop.
Are you sad is not a question but a way of life.
I feel myself floating in the sky looking down for food.
There is Africa from the moon.

FIRST STEP

My ten year old grandson
woke me up from my Sunday
afternoon nap. He
gently put his arms around
me – let me know
that dinner was ready
downstairs. Then he crawled
up on the bed himself
with his back to me
and looked out the window
at the lonely winter trees
trying to make family.
I stirred and sat on the edge
of the bed. He came over to me,
took my arm saying
let me help you, grandpa.
Outside the trees were
fighting a cold wind,
struggling to make sense
of so many changes.
When we reached the
bedroom door
my grandson let go
of my arm, smiled, and said
now, you're on your own.

OBOE SOLO

> *As Van Gogh understood, gold comes*
> *in many forms: the best is art.*
>
> —Madeline DeFrees

She played her chosen
instrument

carefully as if
Mozart might be

guarding his concerto
off-stage.

I came to hear this music
live because of a free ticket

and to keep my own art
from crawling out from under

my skin and away. I was not playing.
The world is *not* so much with us and you can hope

to God your addiction is not to heaven. The saved
still do the stuff

in the right crowd. I watched her
and it was like waiting for the snake

to rise from the basket
and strike.

THE WORKOUT

Shadow boxing
while sitting there at your
desk writing one
word next
to another. Blood
pounding in your ears,
arms pushing weights
to their limit. Sweat
stinging your eyes
as you pace around the ring
gathering strength,
another broken nose.
All the memory gone to anger.
Sister, you need
a punching poem.

CONSTELLATION

I looked up at the high
desert sky
and saw eight
of the seven sisters.
Then your love,
out loud, released
in a moment
which is why I stayed quiet—
discretion being the better
part of distress.

POSTCARD FROM MEXICO

You have traveled the ruins,
danced,
studied the romance
of the words,
and still this love
is as quiet
as paper.

HER MADNESS

I would go raving
mad if the only
person I talked
to all day
was me, pointing
with her hand
to the general area
of her heart. Its
dangerous memory
keeps
her fingers
crossed
a distant second
a good morning
better evening
finally wine.

SLJIVOVICA

You called and said you
would be late
for everything. Then turned
to the small glass
of plum brandy after
talking with a husband who
wants a divorce
and his wife
who doesn't.

She cried, he did not.
She spoke, he was silent.
She won't be touched, he gave up trying.

It seems they are both
late for everything, too, no longer
dizzy in love
just madly dividing up the furniture
and their daughter.

CONCERTINA WIRE

> *-- God bless the child who's got his own....*
> (Holiday and Herzog)

There are two
institutions for the poor:
The military
and prison. In each case
they are surrounded
by circles of gleaming
silver concertina wire.
It is the music of
their place in life
where so often
this and that don't
go the way they ought.
Like today finding
the words, *Kill him?*
in a child's handwriting on stray
paper from the after
school program. One ten year old
girl told me she is
too old to dream any more. The music
continues on little
scraps of paper, notes for a song
from the children of concertina.

THERE'S MORE TO KANSAS

For the second
time this summer
an alligator was found
here in Wichita. Three
to four feet long so they say
it must have been dumped
along the road
by its former owner.
Keep in mind then
that Kansas is much more
than the Wizard
of Oz and Dorothy,
as we mourn
the tragic
passing of Toto.

MEMORIAL DAY

      Kansas – 2005

I went to Spangles for
my Memorial Day
hamburger, fries and
shake. My # was
478 although I
was the only customer.
Alice took my order,
gave me a cup for a coke
but I reminded her
of the chocolate shake.
She apologized. She looked like
she was almost happy
to be there. It was a job, she said,
but it was a job. I did not
know her but could tell
by her face she was
a veteran of many wars.
I order you to give a flag, neatly folded,
to a close relation, twenty-one gun salute, taps
played by a soldier in uniform with a real bugle.
And after she is buried put a small
gravestone on the ground above her to remember
the many assaults she faced
alone with no weapons
or army of support. On the stone put
her last words to me:
Here you go, hun.

FINALLY

When I finally memorized
the spelling of Mediterranean
I believed I knew everything
about the entire sea.

THE TIJUANA CITY DUMP

Nothing special.
Children look as ancient
as recently discovered
stone caves. White
dust whispers lost
virgin soil over the
cardboard beds laid
out for the night. Heavy fog
covers those of us
staring back at you.
Finding a coin or a
stray pear means
everything.

BEING ZEUS

In Memoriam: Kenneth Koch

He is a curious dog. He goes to the trash
in my study and pulls out old poems or fragments
to inspect or chew. Sometimes he seems to know
exactly what he is looking for but usually
he is just – curious. Being the god
of gods is not easy. There is actually
not a lot of independence and so much is
expected of you. Sit for this treat, go
only in the backyard, yes, you have to
be on the leash, don't steal the sandwich
from the kitchen counter, off the couch
I'm here, you're in the way of the television,
the news with roadside bombs and strangled lovers.
Being Zeus during these times is tough, no one
pays any attention even to your thunder
or bolts of lightning. You should try being Venus.

ROSES

Knowing first hand
what it means
to be human
I can fix
sad roses.
How dare you
try to forget.

"CRESCENDO IN BLUE"

I was really
heart beaten when I saw
with my own eyes
the difference between love
and lust. It was a melody
with notes on the page
and then improvisation
which exploded
in my face
as I went out one door,
she another.
That is the crescendo.
Those are the blues.
I've played
the instruments,
given away the children,
talked to the suicidal
teenager, tried to get
families to hear
each other through
the shouting. Now,
to end some war
or take groceries to
one person dying
from emphysema. Or call the one
I love and get no answer, only:

What is happening to my phone?
So much is missed
that wraps us in
its laughter and you thought
you would see each
other today. Try
another dream after
you crawl through this one.

NEAR MISS

Listen as Orpheus
phones the dead
and makes plans
that most have read

or they've seen the film
slip across the screen.
Then a light dress
that most have seen

and enjoyed those legs
shimmering in Hades' light
and the strange fruit
swallowed by the night.

WATCHING THE NEWS

Tonight the dog was wanting to go
for the gutter
every time I let him out. He would
whine and stare at me as I sat in
the red chair trying to watch the news.
He would do that deep throated half-growl
that says – I need the back yard. But then
he would run straight for his special delicacy
which I could not see in the dark. It was cold outside
and beginning to snow. I managed to get him away from
the mystery meal and inside the house
in time to catch a glimpse of the blood on what looked like
the remains of a car on a street in Iraq. Then the news was over.

Woman wins gas for life

And this is the second time.
Of course we are all aware of the double meaning.
As she is.
There is her picture on the front page of the paper.
We have other news but those photos are forbidden.
They would invade the privacy of grieving families.
Might demoralize the troops fighting for liberty.
And undermine public support for democracy.
The woman gets $1200 a year for fifty years of gas.
This seems to be a year for winning at any cost.
This seems to be a year for losing at any cost.
There is another photo on the front page, 20 years old, national guard.
She graduated high school last year, ran track, gave it everything.

MS. TAYLOR

I spent my life
teaching myself to see.
Then with the brush in my mouth
I painted. Sometimes I don't ever need words.
This is no pastoral scene. It is me.
Self-portrait of a naked disabled artist.
That's what I call it. Sometimes I lay the large canvas on the floor
to get the right angle. The neighbors, next to my studio, are on the roof
again to get a look inside.

NIGHT JASMINE

That was your
big mistake. You realized
then its better
to be a little lost
than entirely
found. Resurrection
just means things
are not as they seem.
I keep having
to learn that. Can you
smell the fragrance
from the open window? You think
of a place where the jasmine
would be at home
with you. Watch the live,
tilting-to-one-side
man. He is actually
an angel spinning
on the head
of God. Then you remember
the hawks
were really vultures.

LESSON #9

You say, humans aren't meant to be alone—
although we so often
do such harm when together.

LESSON #10

O, John Clare, so many of us
have died to sing
the songs you taught with courage and madness to love.

BACK THERE

Same active molecule, just slightly different
                side effects.
     Then her smiling eyes
    ask if I hear
what is back there. Back there
            in the pond.
It's them, the leopard frogs! They have
   stripes somewhere on the face,
they keep the night alive just
a little longer, they remind us of the world
           beyond what is found
on any average day. There is the
    immortal. It's just
    not for us.

FIRST STORM

You love to stand out
in the cold wind from
the north at night. It
comes from
Colorado and Wyoming
rattling the windows and giving
you hope in the unknown. You know
you can find a new life, a full
light, in the dark of the clouds
off to the north and
the west. It is a mystery
as she asks about
the snow, has it come
yet…no, life is still
on the move, the snow
is craving a
light falling onto
the ground prepared
for anything but this.
Go back, go back, and you
know it is not possible.
It is still dark in
that direction and
life is on the move
past all that we know.

WHISPERING

yellow finches hang
upside down
to get the seeds

of the sunflower
soon they will be
making circles
in the sky

whispering to each other
better to be present
and visible
than absent
and seen.

THE WOMAN FROM TYRE

She wasn't slouching toward you but knowing your face
from her many dreams and dreads she came full force
shouting for good reason
at what you could and better do.

Then you tried to get out of it claiming
the gift was only
for a select few from the right
country, this was a border issue
but she did not buy it. So she kept shouting
and your friends covered their ears
and told you
to get rid of her,
damn woman,
she lives too close
to the sea,
the salt has made her mad.

But the crowds were also watching as always like they had
digitals and video
so what could you do? It wasn't your gift
to begin with. It really belonged to her
and, thank God, you recognized the truth before
it was too late. So you said, *lady,
because of your love, which we will talk about later,
your daughter will not die. She will live to shout
at some other startled and stumbling savior.*
That's what he said, just ask his friends,
if there are any left.

FIDDLING

One poet writes of the *horse latitudes*
in the calm of the storm. One lover
strikes a fiddle, finds a lonely
instrument of courage with many
ways to be an artist or a scam. You
make the money you make
from your art. Your lover and others
have a name for you but you have their #.

BOSNIAN FOLK SONG

Walking the streets
of Mostar
late and into
the darkness
on the Croat side
of the river
we sing —
absence being a body
like heaven.

DIMMING

Ashes to ashes
    dust to dust
this \\

is what we do with
    trust ---

dim that thought
        like light
            from your eyes

into the oncoming truck
    or train or ---

as you say
    my love of death

remember
    everyone is an adult
  once
a child
    twice.

GLASS

enough for now
love to make it through
the thoughts not regrets
you had after the sharp words
left your tongue
moved across
my body
and scarred both of us
as if the glass from childhood
cut our skin which
we gave to each other.

SECRETS

You are tired
of all
memory.

You are full
to overflowing
with holding

back tiny
child-like
secrets.

REVENGE

For Richard Hugo, In Memory

You can pretty much count on storms flying in
or out of
Denver like today. Waiting
on the runway as 4 p.m.
darkness blocks our
way to the southwest
and on to Los Angeles.
The pilot talks to the tower.
There must be a way
out and around
the weather. Is there some
message hidden
in this text?
You have the window seat
and write like crazy,
Plath's last day's
worth of frantic poems
because you are trying
to forget how
badly you have
to pee. The two
teenage girls in center
and aisle are asleep.
Others get to go do what they want to do!
You did not choose this seat,
did not pay for this journey.

You were sent, it's part of the job
and you can only afford so much revenge
unlike Brahms toasting the Indians
after Little Big Horn.

A COLD SPRING

The lilacs bloom like the mouth of a long, wild cry.
The fragrance gives the air a cup.
It overflows like the swallowed soft-shell star.
The blossoms, though so much of the world, still appear abandoned.
They are silent under a cold midnight sky.
In the morning they come to church, blessing in their Lenten way, our wild love.

LAST THERAPY BEFORE BOSNIA

The clouds break
as I walk
out the door.
Transference
was working
overtime. Then
she put her hand
on my shoulder, told me
how courageous I was, to be
safe, send emails and write down
the next appointment.

I DREAM OF WHINING

Too old for this shit –
men, women, all like the rest of us
mixing messages for those
we love to confuse
each other. Is there any
other way to fall in
love? It just always… you know
it does, and the timing is so wrong flowers
don't help. And try
giving them away on the street
to people you don't
know. They looked at me like
I was some Vodka-crazed gutter
person. I know you have heard this story
before and you even sound bored
between bites
of tortilla chips but that is also why
with such passion I wanted
Sarajevo. It was so much
safer than any lover
with metaphor and logic
that once again forced my heart
to its impotent knees.

LATE WINTER

You've had enough. What
was taken for love
has turned everything inside
out. The inch of snow
meant to wake us up
this morning
never came. The sun
through the window
proclaims a moratorium
on love and darkness.

THE WAR GAME

And the stones
whirl like we are told
the planets must
do above the enemy waiting with carved
wooden guns. The ambush
is set and we are in position to be trapped
and, yes, imagine the stories that will be told
by the victors. That is the way of history,
of conquering heroes. The days fly like the snap
of slingshots and the nights draw lines around
our breathing. It is filth we lie in as we
await our narrated death. Boys being boys. Some follow,
a few lead. In the end it makes no difference
for as we wait the larger artillery is moved into place.
Our mother's cherished babies will all be lost,
unrecognized in the ditches, covered with mud among leaves.

VIGIL

If it wasn't for the last minute
so much would never get done.
There is something about the closing
moment of possibility, a final
shot from beyond
the 3-point line, the words
I have to leave now, and
remembering my mother's
four days of last
breath. In that case
not much was done except
a building exhaustion that eight
years later seems to be easing
but who can trust
what may crash through again
anytime? Best to watch
the glass and gold angel that hangs
by a thread from her I.V. stand
above the bed. The angel
will bless her and you, the dead
and the living,
in that last minute —
the withering away of
body and breath —
all friends emptied from
the folded and torn map of prayer —
if I die before I wake —
by a thread.

SOMETHING ABOUT MY LIFE

When I was in high school I read Poe,
Freud, a book on Matthew's gospel, and others
on politics. None were assigned, they came
from visits to the town library. I started collecting
records of jazz greats and famous symphonies. I ran
miles and miles down the coast from Oceanside
or east out to Mission San Luis Rey, the queen
of oppression and soul saving. I was almost very good.
After the workouts which I usually did by myself,
preferred it that way, yes, all that delicious loneliness,
I went to the library to breathe and smell something
about my life. It was soon time to go to the city
bus stop at Mission and Hill Streets. I rode with
the few – young and scared – marines and their wives
or daughters back to Camp Pendleton, home for the night.
I was the only one to get off in the darkness at the road
I walked leading to the house at the top of Wire Mountain.

January 25

The wolf moon
  white teeth
  blackened gums
a howling of the eyes

I remember my father
steering the car
with so much
   grace

like the owl
gliding across
  the road
  in anticipation
  of whatever
reflection startled the light

   and how
the police helicopter circles
  tonight with its eye
  on the houses and backyards
of my neighborhood

on the human violence
  done tonight

    down the street
  under the full
      wolf moon, white teeth
      gnashing and

howling until sunrise.

END RHYME

It doesn't feel like the day after Christmas
on our night flight to Dallas. Towns below
shine like clusters of stars or swirling
galaxies the names of which I'll never know.

The wings of the plane are visible in the dark,
the window reflects this page of my notebook. Take
your time in standing up for hope, you may find
yourself stung by the spider, poisoned by the snake.

This document should be retained as evidence
of your journey. Bless the ones making love
like the world will end tomorrow. Then sing
the Sanctus, lock the dead bolt, release the dove.

MY SURROUNDINGS (PART 1)

On my writing desk
is a photograph of Cora, Anna and Elleke, two
daughters, one granddaughter. Just to the right is a
photo I took of the skyline of Sarajevo
in 2003 and a postcard from a friend
with Martin Luther King's picture. Then a card sent by Anna
on Father's Day. It is entitled, "Mary and Morris Shaving"
    and refers
to the time in Montana when I taught in a two-room school.
    For show
and tell I got all ten kids into or near the bathroom and I shaved.
There was no time at home, on the ranch, to shave so I
    brought with me what I
needed. Anna was in that class, first grade and remembered —
so in her note on the card she wrote, *Elleke demands a repeat
performance sometime in the not too distant future years!*
All of this is part of what surrounds me. There is more
for another time. Tonight I am content
and filled like only a father can be filled to read
Anna's other words, *it's been so wonderful to have you
in our lives & our home & and as my dad & as Elleke's grandpa
Mike. We love you! Anna & the mini girl.*
There is a lifetime here in my study, maybe just
on the desk. It is chaos until each item is looked at
and named. Does it take a clever line or phrase
to close this poem and give it the punch that makes

it more than observation or, God forbid, prose?
Then listen carefully, as I am doing, trying to return
to this past Christmas when Cora was smiling yet so sick,
Anna stood tall in her beauty and Elleke noticed the ceramic
figure on the top of a large piece of furniture and said, *fish*.
Did you hear her? All of this, and more, surrounds me.

THE NOISE OF PLANTS

You walked near the
morning garden
and heard the sound
of the flowers waking
to each other, offering
coffee, a slice of toast,
a smile saying
come back to bed.
That's where it ended.
With the frown
of whatever was lost
somewhere deep
in the earth.

HOPE

It is Prague
and raining. You
speak the cold language
in the bars and on the street.
Taste this.

Hear the church
bells. They call to you
for peace, for a sober
night.

Then morning brings the lonely
quiet of the empty
sanctuary and a soft breeze
across the river, the bridge,
along the castle wall

where you stand
still waiting
with your candle.

THE DANCE

It takes so much strength
and grace
like a ballet
to stay
alive in this kitchen.
A few flowers and a box of fancy knives
on the counter with several
days of newspapers
scattered around the room as if blown
by the wind.
Then the finale, legs still,
arms moving slowly down
to the hips. The music
ends with a quiet single string
and the dance
concludes
with an arm around the neck
of one man.

SARAJEVO SYMPHONY

It's early in the evening
and I am glad. No
rush to the darkness
or a room filled
with dreams and wishes
disappearing with the
music. It is fear
and as the cello moans
like someone in quiet pain
I tuck myself between the
bed and the wall. I can hear
the morning radio news
and breathe easy again in spite
of more deaths in my daylight.
No love lost. No
love. My life is one more
humanitarian agency
pulling out because of bombs
in the plaza. Down the street
the quick response to
emergency calls suddenly
brings into question where
the bullet entered, where did
the bullet exit, when will
revenge visit this home,
whose blood is whose.

STRANGE FRUIT

(Beslan, Russia, 2004)

Here at School Number 1
you see the excitement
of the young children
on their first day. Also
the tears of parents,
their reluctance to let them
go like small apples
gently released by
the tree. They will
become ripe so very soon
as the bright red season
will come like an explosion
of color
early this fall.

SCHOOL IN SUDAN

At eight years old they took me away but taught me many things.
First, how to shoot the AK-47.
Then how to build a good fire and to cook for myself.
How to bury and arm land mines.
Then we were taught how to attack a village.
And then we learned how to quickly fall back.
Finally, they taught us not to think about the dead.

NOT A FAIRY TALE

The war is door to door.
You could stand only so much with
the stench of lively children
thrown into the ditch. You fill
the empty brandy glasses, keep
the shovels moving while it is still dark
and the sky is drunk with plums.

THE HOUSE

You lived just off the kitchen.
Anyone could come through
or watch what you were doing
from three different rooms. Your mind
could drift, too, into the living room
or the bathroom. The kitchen.
Your thoughts could create a meal,
an argument, or brush your hair.
Your fantasies could swirl
through the house like a magic scarf
in the wind. You could imagine
anything with wild leaps of the heart
without thought of those killing headaches.
They've been coming more often. The doctor
offers more drugs. You prefer scotch.
You prefer screaming with your eyes
at me. You prefer not expecting too much.

WEATHERED

During these
Kansas storms
I wonder what it is
like for Florence,
Loretta, Elmer,
and all the others
who have lost
those people they had
cringed with
for so many years
in dark rooms.

THE YEARS

This is the season
for the shoulders
to curve
forward. Each step
a time to gather
breath. The bad thing is
you are always looking
down and may see
a coin far,
far away.

SUNDAY'S COMIN'

—Walk with me, Lord

the birds were eating
and singing
eating and singing
a meadowlark
invisible to your
eyes called to someone
in the trees
or the sky
soon the last layers
of daylight
corner you in
an orange world
where you can sing
a blue rage
in the face
of such blind silence
you pinch yourself
in disbelief

Michael Poage was born in Virginia and has lived in New England, California, Montana and overseas in Latvia and Bosnia and Herzegovina. He has ten collections of poems published prior to this new book. He worked various jobs before becoming ordained in the United Church of Christ and serving three congregations in Kansas. He has also taught at Friends University, Wichita State University, the University of Latvia and Dzemal Bijedic University in Mostar, Bosnia and Herzegovina, where he also served as Poet-in-Residence in 2017-18. When not in Bosnia and Herzegovina, he and his wife, the historian and writer, Dr. Gretchen Eick, live in Wichita, Kansas.

This project was made possible, in part, by generous support from the Osage Arts Community.

Osage Arts Community provides temporary time, space and support for the creation of new artistic works in a retreat format, serving creative people of all kinds — visual artists, composers, poets, fiction and nonfiction writers. Located on a 152-acre farm in an isolated rural mountainside setting in Central Missouri and bordered by ¾ of a mile of the Gasconade River, OAC provides residencies to those working alone, as well as welcoming collaborative teams, offering living space and workspace in a country environment to emerging and mid-career artists. For more information, visit us at www.osageac.org

Osage Arts Community

www.ingramcontent.com/pod-product-compliance
Lightning Source LLC
Chambersburg PA
CBHW020126130526
44591CB00032B/545